UNCLE SAM'S BIRTHDAY
1776 JULY 4TH 1976
200 YEARS YOUNG
GREETINGS FROM
NASHVILLE
TENNESSEE
I0824122

AMERICAN REVOLUTION BICENTENNIAL 1776-1976
"It is probably a pity that every citizen of each State
cannot visit all the others, to see the differences,
to learn what we have in common, and to come back
with a richer, fuller understanding of America."
Dwight D. Eisenhower

76
Me, age 8

MY BICENTENNIAL SUMMER

True Adventures from the Most Epic Family Road Trip of All Time

G. Neri

illustrated by Corban Wilkin

Candlewick Press

First edition 2026

Library of Congress Control Number: pending
ISBN 978-1-5362-3957-7

CCP 31 30 29 28 27 26
10 9 8 7 6 5 4 3 2 1

Printed in Shenzhen, Guangdong, China

This book was typeset in Ankesans.
The illustrations were created digitally.

Candlewick Press
99 Dover Street
Somerville, Massachusetts 02144

www.candlewick.com

EU Authorized Representative: HackettFlynn Ltd,
36 Cloch Choirneal, Balrothery, Co. Dublin, K32 C942, Ireland.
EU@walkerpublishinggroup.com

Trying to stay dry at Niagara Falls!

Me and bros at Painted Desert

On board tall ship in NY Harbor

For my family

Concord Minutemen with Dad's friend B

Waiting at the White House for the president

As a kids' author, I get to travel all over America. In fact, I've been to forty-eight of the fifty states doing school visits or research for my books! And because my travels have also taken me as far away as Antarctica, Siberia, and the Zulu region of South Africa, kids always ask me:

You see, all my stories begin from some experience I've had out on the road, visiting someplace I had never been to, where I've stumbled across something I'd never seen, heard of, or experienced before.

And usually, my reaction is something like this:

which can sometimes lead to a reaction like this:*

*actual reader of my first book!

This book that you are holding now is no exception. It's the story of how I first learned to look at the world like an explorer. You see, it all started from a family road trip I took when I was a kid, a long, long time ago . . .

The year was 1976. That's right—I was a kid before smartphones, Wi-Fi, or streaming even existed. We didn't even have a computer!

I grew up in Southern California, and like most kids there, when I wasn't in school, I was either watching TV (three channels!), reading comics, or riding my skateboard.

Back then, it felt like America was in a slump. We'd just gotten out of a bad war in Vietnam, had stopped sending astronauts to the moon, and had a president resign from the White House in disgrace. People were having a hard time finding jobs, and prices were going up everywhere! Americans weren't feeling very patriotic.

But all that was about to change . . .

Because on July 4th, 1976, America was going to have the Biggest Baddest Birthday Party *EVER!* We were going to be 200 years old—a national birthday so humongous it had its own name: *the Bicentennial*.

The entire year leading up to it, the American Bicentennial was *everywhere*. On TV . . . on billboards . . . in newspapers and magazines . . . even on clothes!

Two hundred years before, back in 1776, America had declared independence against that tyrant, King George III of the British Empire (*Booo!*). We were tired of having to pay taxes for things that had nothing to do with us (like a war against France). We wanted our freedom!

I'd learned about all sorts of moments from America's fight for independence in school:

The Boston Massacre and the Tea Party revolt

Paul Revere's midnight ride

Washington crossing the Delaware

The colonial troops barely surviving the winter at Valley Forge

Betsy Ross making the US flag

That treacherous traitor Benedict Arnold

But the biggest moment of all was the signing of the Declaration of Independence in Philadelphia!

We hold these truths to be self-evident, that all men are created equal, that they are endowed by their Creator with certain unalienable Rights, that among these are Life, Liberty and the pursuit of Happiness.

In 1976, I didn't know what all that meant, but it sounded important.

Me and my two older brothers totally bought into the Bicentennial hype, despite the fact that, as the only kids of color at our school, we sometimes didn't feel like real red, white, and blue Americans.

I'd never thought too much about the meaning behind the Pledge of Allegiance. Sure, we said it every morning, but who knew what those words really meant? They were just old ideas our teachers made us say.

But there was no denying the Spirit of '76 that year. My whole family caught Bicentennial fever, and one day after New Year's, my mom had this wild idea:

Up to that point, the biggest trip we ever took was a day's drive up to Lake Shasta to stay in a houseboat. This was something entirely different.

Where would we eat? Where would we sleep? How would we survive seven hours a day in the car without killing each other?

We laid out a big map of the country and started looking at possible routes.
If we head through the Southwest, we'll be traveling past all the big national parks . . .
Then we could travel through the South to see your brother in Texas . . .
Then up through the thirteen original colonies for all our big Bicentennial sites . . .
before heading back through the heartland . . .

As our fingers traced possible roads to all these famous places, suddenly I could picture us as pioneers like Daniel Boone or Lewis and Clark lighting out for the territories . . .

Or marching like the Minutemen along secret routes to ambush the redcoats in the Revolutionary War!

We were gonna have an adventure—and see history up close and personal.

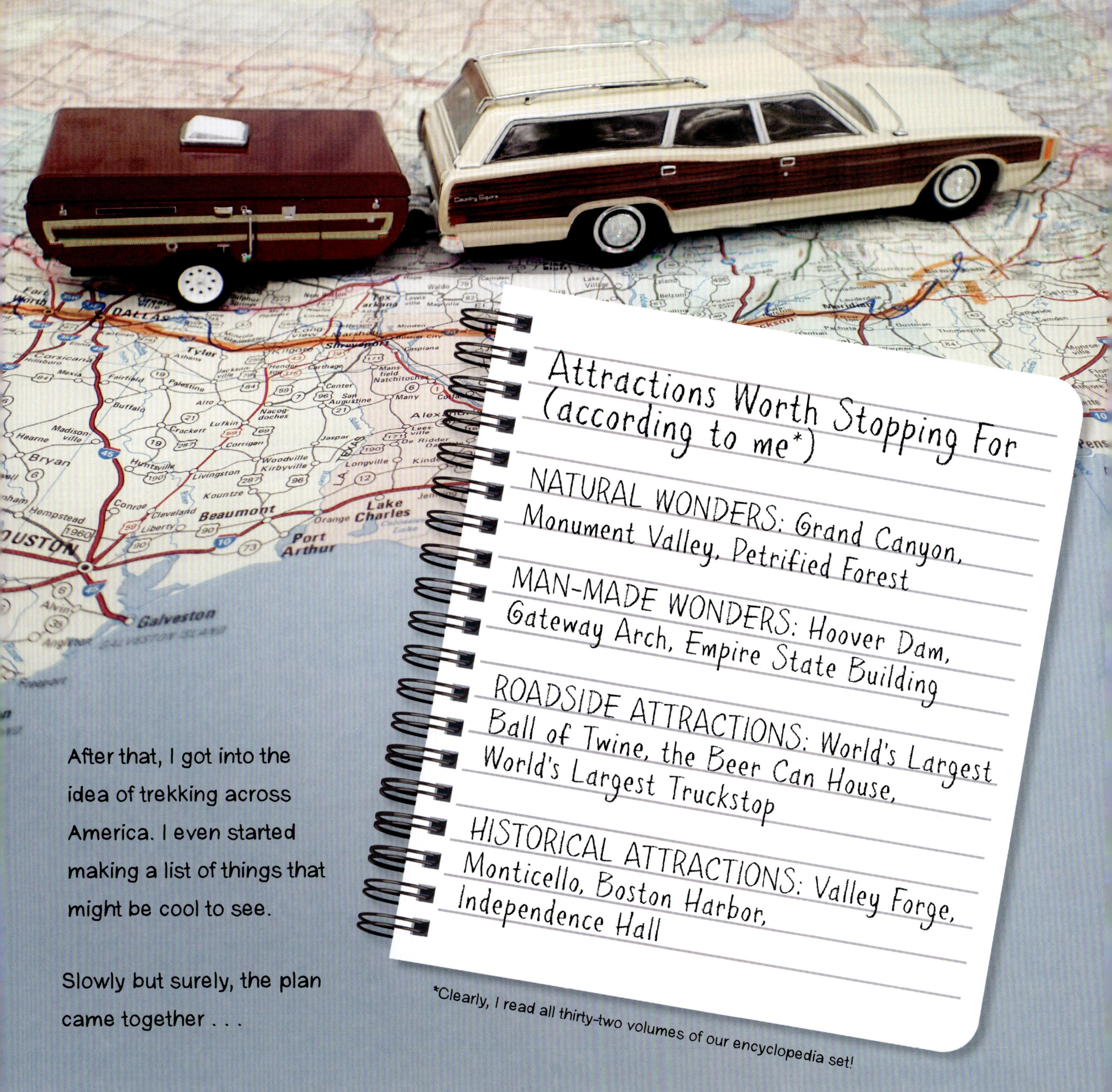

After that, I got into the idea of trekking across America. I even started making a list of things that might be cool to see.

Slowly but surely, the plan came together . . .

*Clearly, I read all thirty-two volumes of our encyclopedia set!

OUR TRIP!
(or Around the Country in 52 Days!)

THE MISSION

To drive almost 8,000 miles through twenty-six states in about seven weeks, hitting all the big Bicentennial sites and events, the national parks and monuments, battlefields, and important historical markers that make up America. We might even see a relative or two. The big highlight would be celebrating the Fourth of July in our nation's capital!

OUR ROUTE

1. Los Angeles, CA
2. Lake Havasu, AZ
3. Grand Canyon
4. Meteor Crater
5. White Sands, NM
6. Denton, TX
7. Dallas, TX
8. Little Rock, AR
9. Great Smoky Mountains
10. Charlotte, NC
11. Yorktown, VA
12. Richmond, VA
13. Washington, DC
14. Gettysburg, PA
15. Philadelphia, PA
16. New York, NY
17. Boston, MA
18. Concord, MA
19. Niagara Falls, NY
20. Chicago, IL
21. St. Louis, MO
22. Denver, CO
23. Moab, UT
24. Las Vegas, NV
25. Los Angeles, CA

CANADA
USA
CHICAGO
6
7
8
9
10
11
12
13
14
15
16
17
18
19
20
21
TAMPA, FLORIDA
(Adult Greg lives here)
BEACH TIME!
ATLANTIC OCEAN
GULF OF MEXICO

THE VEHICLE

A car that could get us across deserts, over mountains, through cities, storms, and burning heat . . . That's right, I'm talking about our 1967 wood-paneled Ford Country Squire station wagon* (10 miles to the gallon) equipped with an Apache Eagle pop-up tent trailer!

*I'd sit in the wayback, which was ideal for spying on other cars. And by the way, nobody wore seat belts in the '70s. It's a miracle we all survived!

THE A-TEAM

DAD
Accountant. Korean War veteran. Calm. Quiet. Dad jokes.

MOM
Nurse. Motherly. Claims to not remember our childhood.

ROG
Ten years old. The oldest. The rebel. The surfer.

MATT
Nine years old. The middle brother. Like Peter from *The Brady Bunch*.

ME
Eight years old. The sensitive artist. The record keeper.

MY UNIFORM AND TOOLS

For this kind of mission, special uniforms and tools were required:

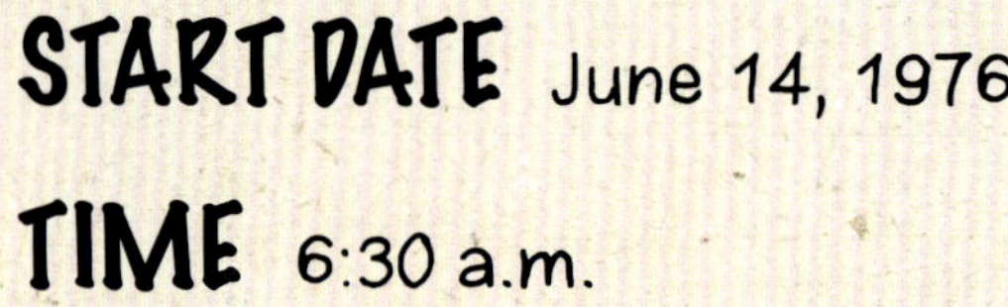

START DATE June 14, 1976

TIME 6:30 a.m.

When the big day came, we were packed and ready to go!

Wallet? Check.

Maps? Check.

Snacks? Check.

See you soon *sniff*... We're coming back...

We sadly said goodbye to our cat, Scratchy (don't worry—our neighbors were taking care of him).

We left our home in Los Angeles behind, and within a few hours, we were on a lonely stretch of highway through the barren heat trap called the Mojave Desert (cue vultures and tumbleweeds).

It was clear right away we were no longer in Southern California. We saw things I'd never seen before:
You mean a meteor hit Earth right here??
METEOR CRATER
What is London Bridge doing in the desert?
LAKE HAVASU

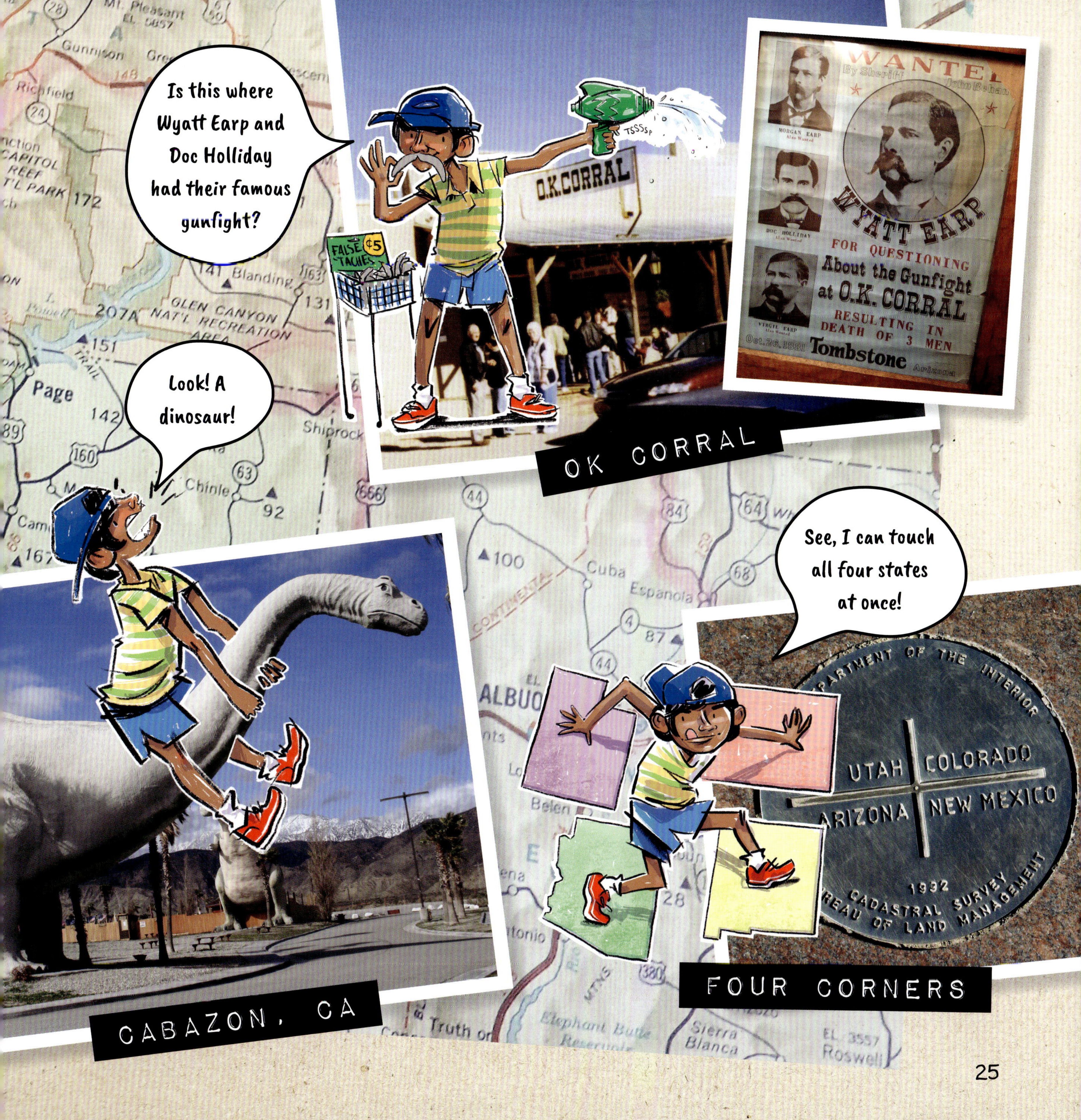

Is this where Wyatt Earp and Doc Holliday had their famous gunfight?
FALSE TACHES ¢5
O.K. CORRAL
WANTED
By Sheriff John Behan
MORGAN EARP
DOC HOLLIDAY
VIRGIL EARP
WYATT EARP
FOR QUESTIONING
About the Gunfight
at O.K. CORRAL
RESULTING IN
DEATH OF 3 MEN
Oct. 26, 1881
Tombstone
Arizona
OK CORRAL
Look! A dinosaur!
CABAZON, CA
See, I can touch all four states at once!
DEPARTMENT OF THE INTERIOR
UTAH
COLORADO
ARIZONA
NEW MEXICO
1992
CADASTRAL SURVEY
BUREAU OF LAND MANAGEMENT
FOUR CORNERS

Whoa...

Each day, we set out with a new destination in mind, but how it would actually play out was a complete unknown. Weather, accidents, running out of gas, or someone getting carsick could change our course at any moment.

We didn't have GPS or cell phones to call ahead to reserve a campsite or motel room. We had to calculate the journey the old-fashioned way: on a paper map, and sometimes using a compass! We usually stopped only when my dad got tired of dealing with us.

To entertain ourselves on the road, we played games like:

When you drive across America, you quickly get an idea how big it is. But as the days went on, it started to feel endless!

At truck stops, we started hearing people talk in all kinds of accents with words we had never used.

Me and my brothers would scour the parking lots looking for license plates from faraway places: Texas, Illinois, Florida, Massachusetts, Washington—even Alaska and Hawaii! Just like us, people were road-tripping from all over the country.

THE HISTORY OF THE AMERICAN ROAD TRIP

1903

First person to drive across the United States: Horatio Jackson, on a bet

1913

Announcement of the treacherous coast-to-coast Lincoln Highway

1927

First 7-Eleven store: Dallas, TX

1929

First highway rest stop: Michigan

582·A6D
LAND OF LINCOLN
JX 9817
19 ILLINOIS 74

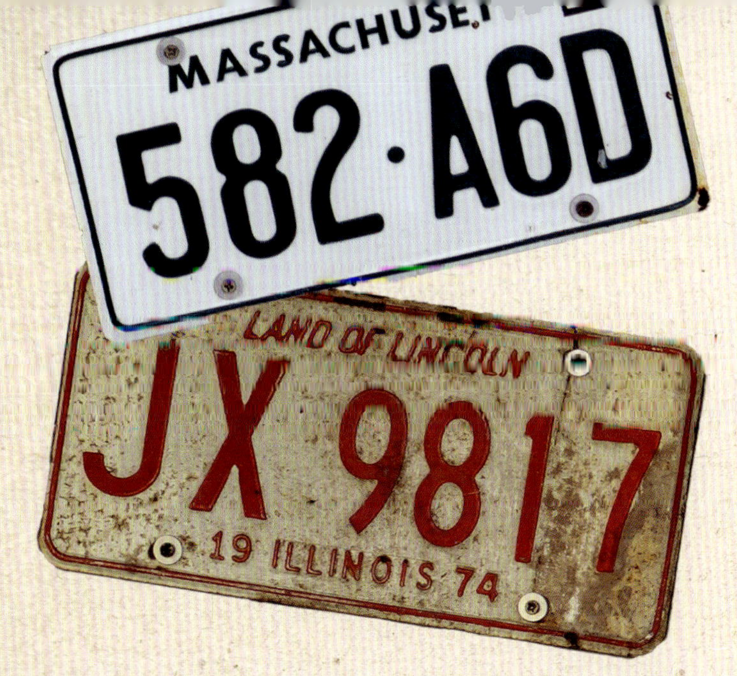

Nowadays, driving across America might not seem so unusual. Heck, I've driven across in four days when I was in a hurry. But back then, road trips were the new way of seeing the country from sea to shining sea. Gas was cheap (59 cents a gallon!), there were plenty of nice rest stops and drive-throughs, and the roads were mostly newly paved!

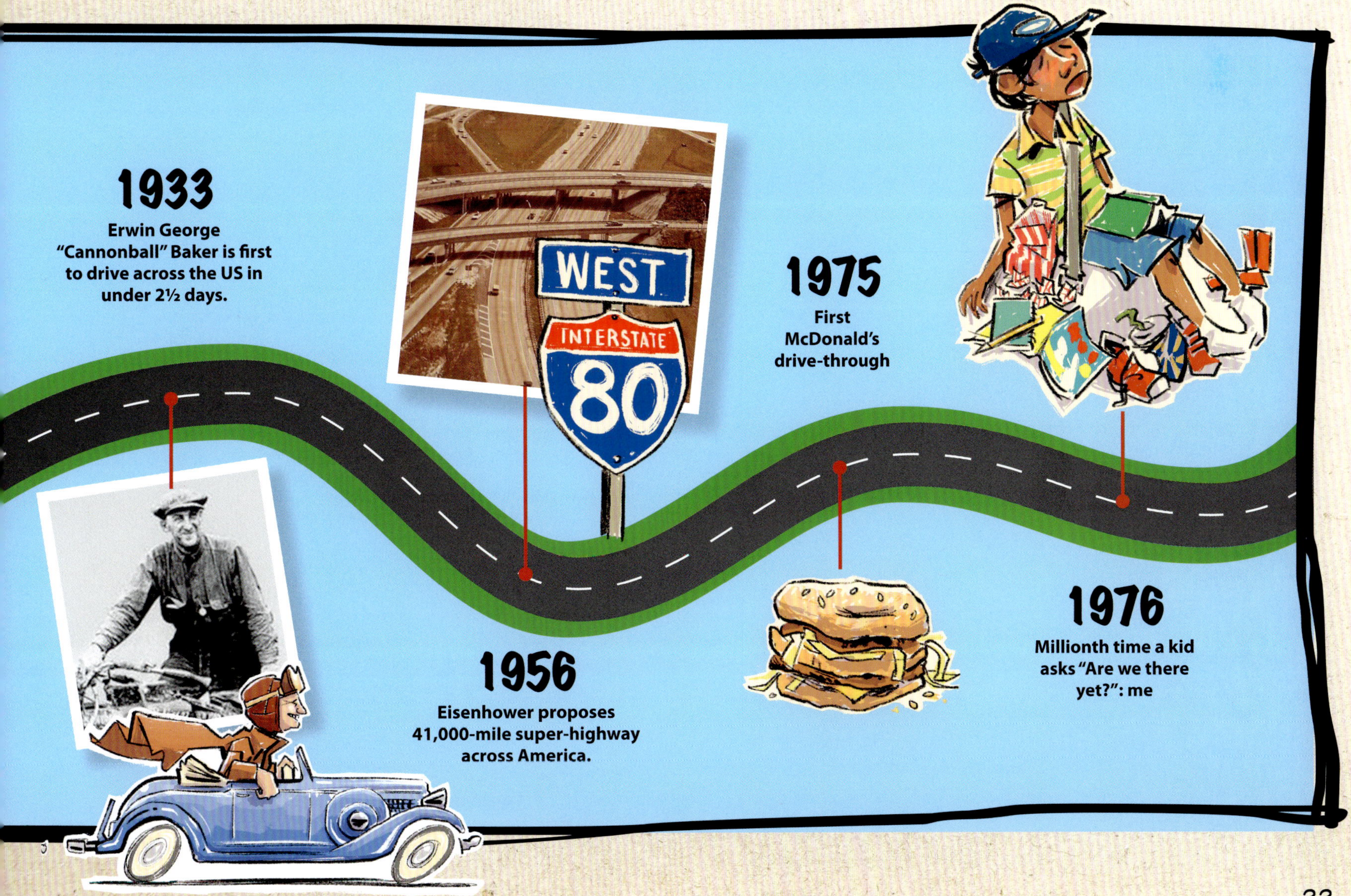
1933
Erwin George "Cannonball" Baker is first to drive across the US in under 2½ days.
WEST
INTERSTATE
80
1956
Eisenhower proposes 41,000-mile super-highway across America.
1975
First McDonald's drive-through
1976
Millionth time a kid asks "Are we there yet?": me

But in between stops, America seemed so empty. I had only seen this kind of alien landscape in the movies. But when you see these wide open spaces in person, you start to think maybe America IS a movie, splayed across the biggest screen you ever saw.

We were only a week into our trip, but I marveled at the endless blue skies, those towering white clouds, and majestic red rocks. It was hot and barren; it felt completely different from Los Angeles. Mirages rose off the heat of the blacktop; lizards, snakes, and scorpions awaited you if you had to wander off for a roadside pee. But at night, it cooled off and everything changed again. Who knew there really was a Milky Way up there!

We saw some pretty cool things along the way. We stopped at Billy the Kid's grave. At the Petrified Forest, my brothers found some real old black arrowheads right on the ground! We rode a mule at the Grand Canyon and later dove off giant white sand dunes. I even got to put my hand inside a dinosaur's footprint!

To document our expedition, I took as many Polaroids as I could. These days, we're used to seeing photos appear instantly on our phones, but back then, it was like magic. You took a picture, and *BZZZT*—it spit out a photo sandwiched between plastic layers of chemicals that developed the image. You had to wait one whole minute (or 60 *Mississippi*s) before peeling off the cover, and then a picture slowly but miraculously appeared. It was pretty rad for 1976.

We camped or stayed in cheap motels most the time, but sometimes we couldn't find a KOA campground or Motel 6, and we'd end up sleeping in a church parking lot. I guess our hardship didn't compare to those pioneers who perished in the olden days, like the Donner Party or people fleeing the Dust Bowl to move out West. Still, me and my two brothers had to share one tiny side of the pop-up tent. Talk about roughing it!

THE TEXAS COUSINS

We took a detour to meet our first Texans. Oddly enough, we were related to them! They were half-cousins on my mom's side, so they really didn't look like us. We'd never visited them before, but it seemed like a good excuse since we were in the neighborhood.

Everything seemed bigger in Texas, including my extended family. They had thirteen kids (!), ten of whom were boys (!!), most of whom were wrestlers (!!!). The boys all slept out in the fields in a separate bunkhouse where midnight surprise attacks were the norm. They would do crazy things like lure us out into a wide-open field, then shoot a real arrow straight up into the high noon sun and run! We figured that's how they do it in Texas.

PS: One of the three girls would grow up to be a horse trainer whom I'd write about in my book *Grand Theft Horse*. But that didn't happen until I met her again much later as an adult!

After Texas, we were officially in "the South." Growing up out West, the only thing we knew about the South was what we saw on TV—you know, good ol' boys, swamps, and cotton. But there was so much more to it than that. We saw Nashville, the home of country music; the mysterious fog of the Great Smoky Mountains; and even some real live alligators!

We had to face some dark things from our country's past, too. We stood on the spot where President Kennedy was killed in Dallas, saw Confederate flags hanging on people's homes, and visited a former slave plantation in Tennessee. I'd heard about Mexican immigrants being rounded up and was worried that I might be grabbed in some rest stop and mistakenly sent south of the border.

We didn't feel so welcome in some places, and one time, a restaurant refused to serve a Black family right in front of us! We left before we were turned away too. But most people were friendly, especially waitresses, who were always calling me *sweetie-pie* and *honey*. Still, my parents seemed uncomfortable and eager to move on.

Even though this trip was supposed to be all about remembering the Revolutionary War, as we traveled through the South, the Civil War kept coming up. By the time we got to Gettysburg, we were all hyped up to re-create Pickett's Charge, where Union soldiers gunned down the charging rebels. We met some kids from Alabama, and it was on!

We played war for a while, but then we heard a real cannon blast and saw men dressed as Union and Confederate soldiers battling it out. Seeing troops getting killed left and right made it feel more real, even if it wasn't.

THE GETTYSBURG ADDRESS

DELIVERED BY ABRAHAM LINCOLN NOV. 19 1863

AT THE DEDICATION SERVICES ON THE BATTLE FIELD

Fourscore and seven years ago our fathers brought forth on this continent a new nation, conceived in liberty, and dedicated to the proposition that all men are created equal. ★★★ Now we are engaged in a great civil war, testing whether that nation, or any nation so conceived and so dedicated, can long endure. ★★ We are met on a great battle-field of that war. ★ We have come to dedicate a portion of that field as a final resting place for those who here gave their lives that that nation might live. ★★ It is altogether fitting and proper that we should do this. ★★ But in a larger sense we cannot dedicate, we cannot consecrate, we cannot hallow this ground. ★ The brave men, living and dead, who struggled here, have consecrated it far above our poor power to add or detract. The world will little note, nor long rem
we say here, but it can never
did here. ★★ It is for us, th
dedicated here to the
who fought here have
It is rather for us t
great task remainin
honored dead we tak
cause for which they
devotion; ★ that we h
these dead shall not h
nation, under God, shal
dom, and that the governme
and for the people, shall not p

When Lincoln himself appeared out of the fog of cannon fire and gave his famous Gettysburg Address, some Black people dressed as slaves were set "free" right in front of us! Suddenly, war didn't seem so fun anymore.

LISTS

All along the way, to keep track of all the amazing and strange things we were seeing, I started making lists. I didn't want to forget, because when school started up again, I would have to do a report on what I did over the summer. Here are the kinds of lists I made:

THINGS YOU WILL/WON'T SEE ON THE ROAD

WILL

- The back of everyone's heads in the car
- Families looking tired or hungry . . . or sometimes having fun together
- Lost people studying paper maps
- Cows and cowboys
- Windmills, barns/silos, fields of corn or cotton
- Eight-track tape players (ask your grandpa)
- Full-service gas stations where attendants check your oil and wash your windows!
- Rest stop vending machines with real ice cream
- Speed traps
- Endless highways

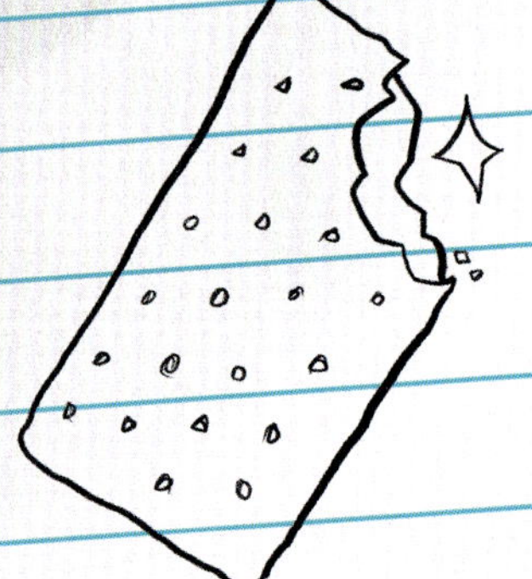

WON'T

- Privacy
- Your own bed
- Your friends
- The beach
- People who dress and talk like you
- Your TV shows
- Places to skateboard
- The snack you were saving for the next stop
- A shower or bathroom that's not gross
- Homework
- Your cat

THINGS I'VE COLLECTED ON THE TRIP

Two-dollar bills and Bicentennial quarters

First edition stamps of fife and drums

Official American Bicentennial patches and pins

Gunslingers' wanted posters (Billy the Kid, Jesse James)

Bottle caps from around the country (RC Cola, Vernors, 7UP, TAB) . . .

A mini Liberty Bell replica

Civil War caps, a Daniel Boone hat, and a Revolutionary War hat

ROADSIDE ATTRACTIONS

Funny billboards that tell a story as you drive

Car sculptures

Rocks shaped like animals

Buildings shaped like clothes

Giants holding wrenches/hot dogs/ tires/axes

Hitchhiker signs

PEOPLE AND THEIR CLOTHES

WEIRD FOOD

Rattlesnake in a can (Texas)

Fried frog legs (Arkansas)

Koolickles: pickles marinated in Kool-Aid (Mississippi)

Head cheese: made from a pig's head (Louisiana)

Brain sandwich: made from a pig's brain (Missouri)

Hot beef sundae (Iowa)

CHURROS

SNAKE

Chitlins, which are cooked pig intestines (Alabama)

THINGS I'VE ONLY SEEN ON TV BEFORE

Cowboys

Hopi Indian kids

Amish buggies

Bison

American eagle

Wild horses

Rocky arches from
another planet

Choppers

Black Minutemen

The real highlights of our Bicentennial trip began when we finally reached the first of the thirteen original colonies in Yorktown, Virginia. There, we saw reenactments of British redcoats surrendering to the colonial forces in full dress. I had some mixed feelings seeing Britain surrender because I loved everything that came out of England (James Bond, Monty Python, the Beatles—*hello?*).

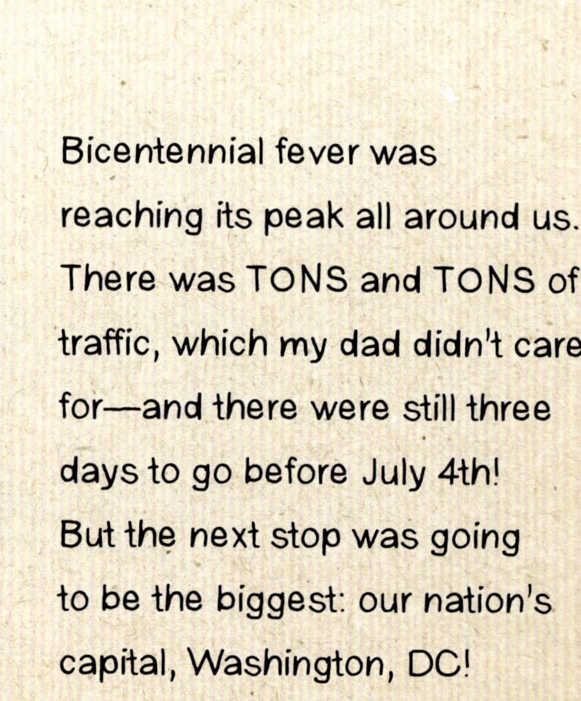

Bicentennial fever was reaching its peak all around us. There was TONS and TONS of traffic, which my dad didn't care for—and there were still three days to go before July 4th! But the next stop was going to be the biggest: our nation's capital, Washington, DC!

I'd never seen a place like DC before. The buildings were old with giant columns. There were cops on horseback riding around the National Mall. And there were a lot of important people in dark suits carrying briefcases. We definitely weren't in California anymore.

Over the next couple of days, we saw everything we could, braving crowds and lines to see the Jefferson Memorial, the Washington Monument, the National Mall, the new National Air and Space Museum, the Lincoln Memorial, and the White House itself!

And then, after waiting in line for what seemed like hours, I found myself face-to-face with the actual Declaration of Independence *and* the Constitution!

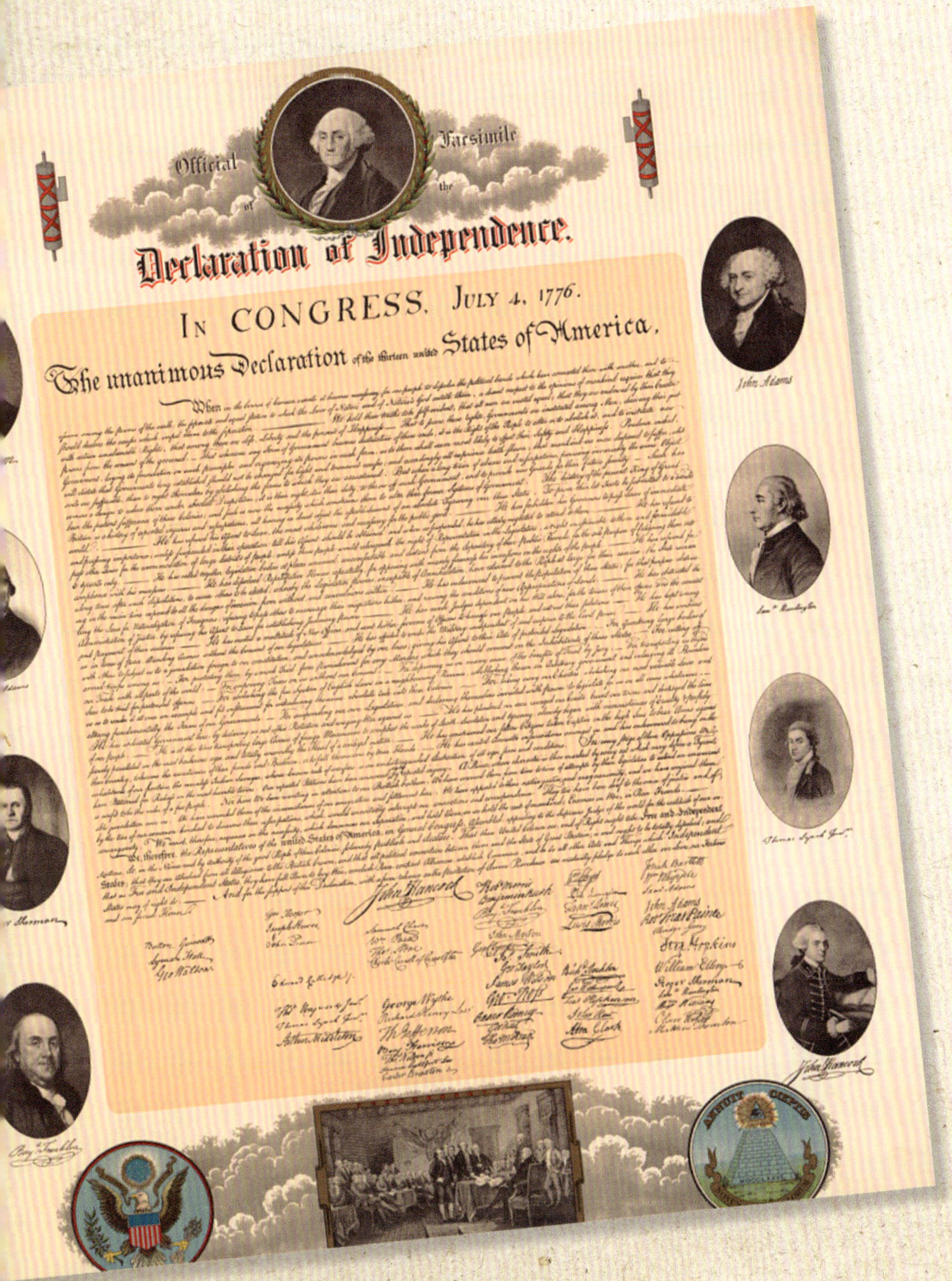

I stared at these ancient pieces of paper in their glass cases and imagined our founding fathers arguing about what beliefs and rules to include. These documents were filled with all kinds of pie-in-the-sky ideas about equality and freedoms that felt a little off to me because when they wrote them, Native Americans were being killed and pushed off their land, most Black people in America were enslaved, and women had almost no rights.

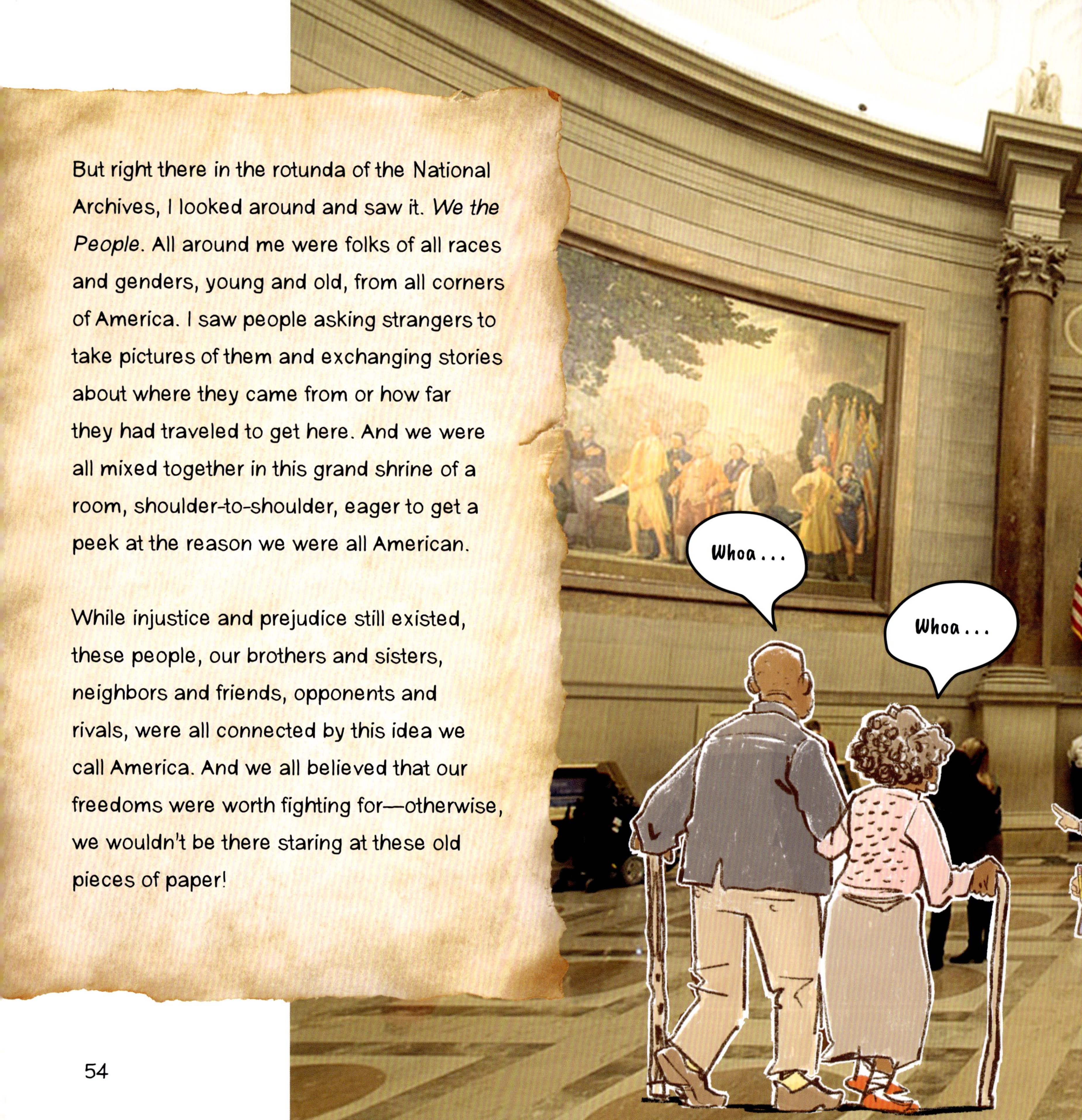

But right there in the rotunda of the National Archives, I looked around and saw it. *We the People*. All around me were folks of all races and genders, young and old, from all corners of America. I saw people asking strangers to take pictures of them and exchanging stories about where they came from or how far they had traveled to get here. And we were all mixed together in this grand shrine of a room, shoulder-to-shoulder, eager to get a peek at the reason we were all American.

While injustice and prejudice still existed, these people, our brothers and sisters, neighbors and friends, opponents and rivals, were all connected by this idea we call America. And we all believed that our freedoms were worth fighting for—otherwise, we wouldn't be there staring at these old pieces of paper!

Whoa...
Whoa...
Whoa...

That night, we found out that DC's big Bicentennial parade would be on July 3rd instead of the 4th. We'd driven almost three thousand miles to celebrate our nation's birthday in its capital. But it gave my dad another idea:

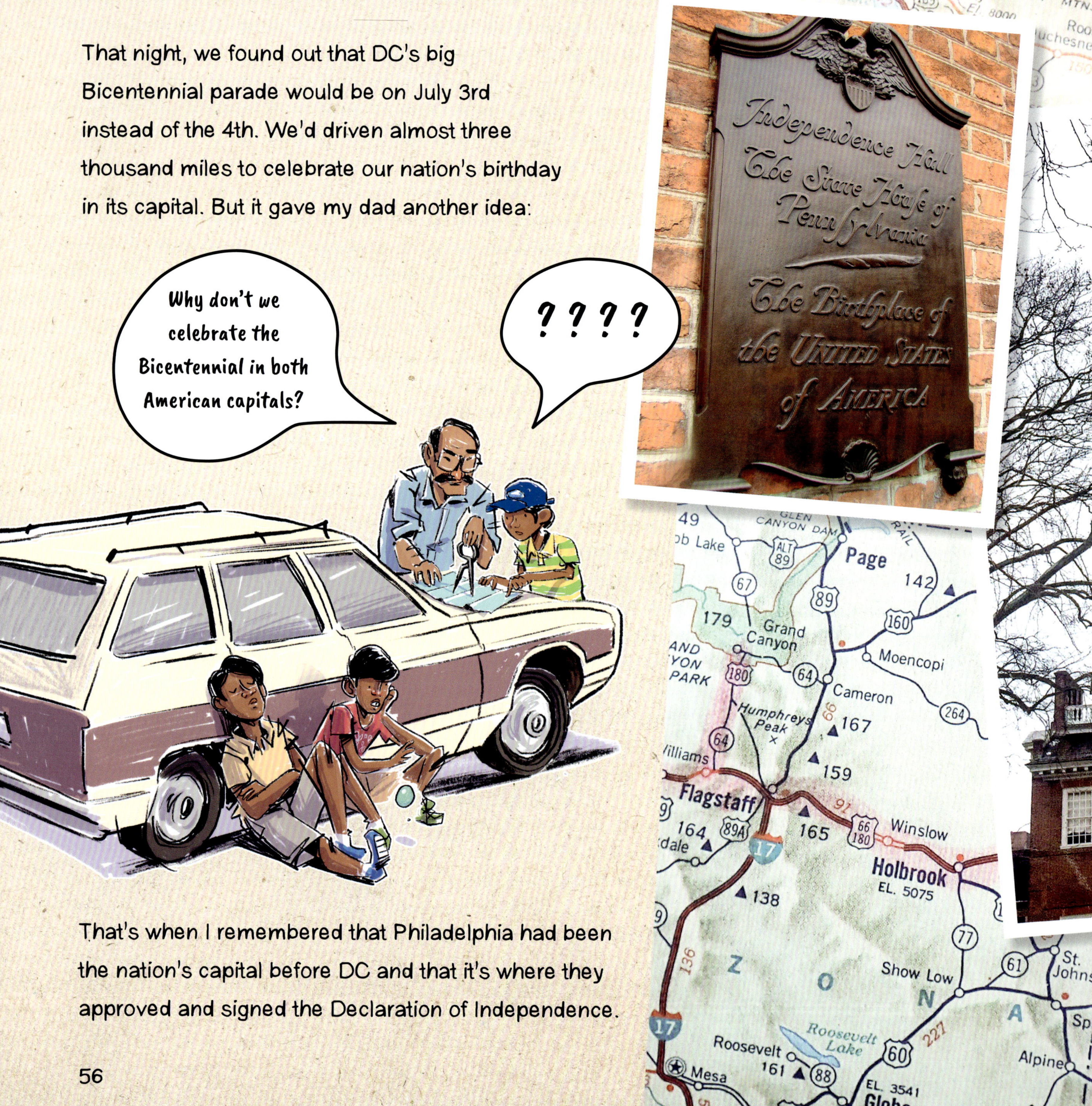

That's when I remembered that Philadelphia had been the nation's capital before DC and that it's where they approved and signed the Declaration of Independence.

Two capitals in two days? We heard the queen of England was planning to visit both cities later in the week, so why not us?

I think my mom was about done with Washington anyway, and this sounded like the ultimate celebration to me! We heard on the news that Philly was planning the biggest parade of all—five hours long with more than forty thousand marchers! We decided to go for it.

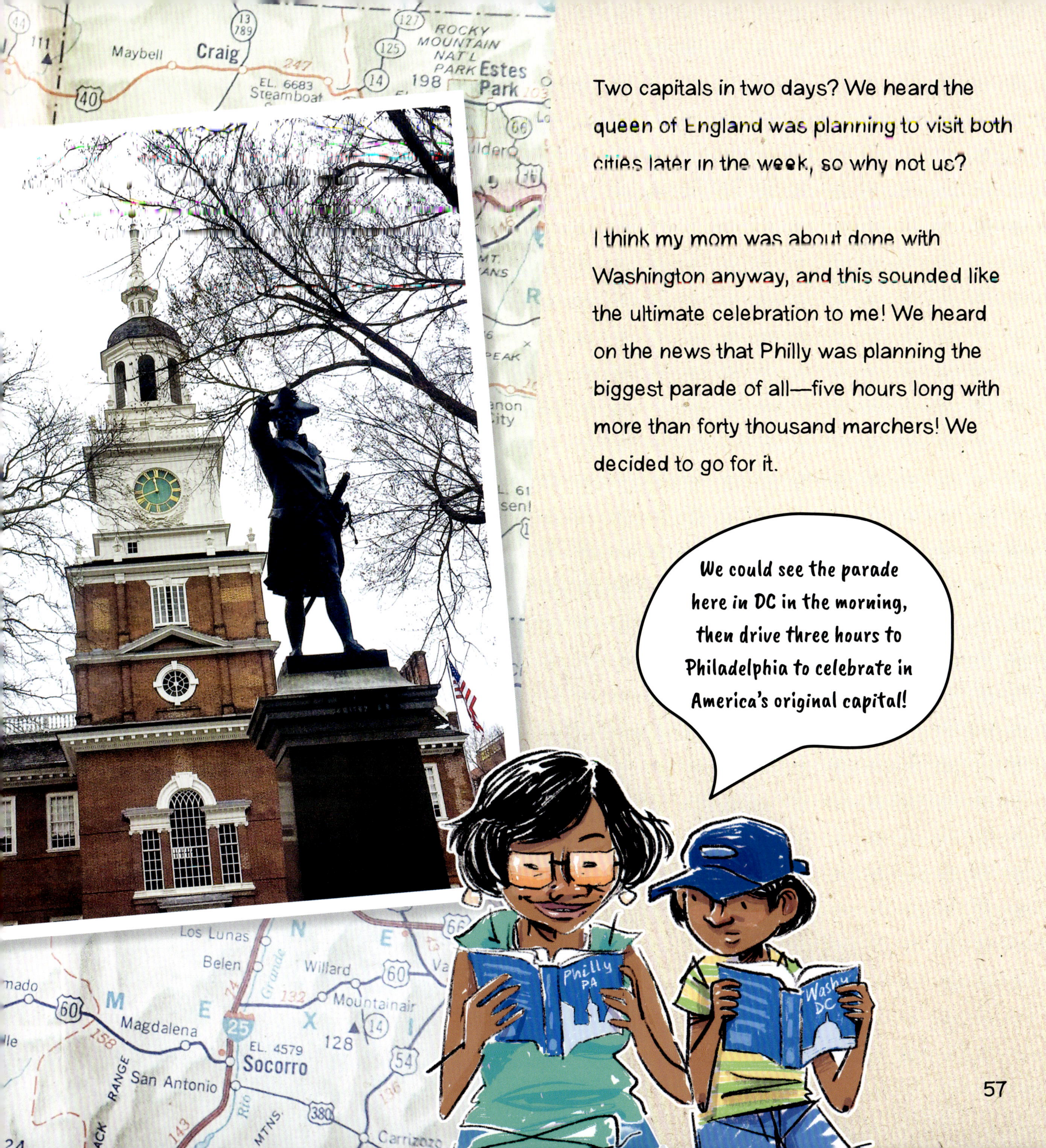

That morning, we battled huge crowds to see DC's stupendous, amazing Fourth of July parade! Johnny Cash, America's favorite country singer, was its grand marshal. We heard half a million people showed up that day, the biggest crowd ever in DC!

Everyone seemed excited about celebrating America's birthday. There were marching bands from almost every state, groups dressed like redcoats and Washington's army, Scottish pipers and Irish dancers, and even a group of Navajo marines from World War II.

By the afternoon, we were all paraded out, so we jumped in our car and sped (more like crawled) northeast, toward Bicentennial City: Philadelphia!

Unfortunately, we arrived along with *two million* other people, so there was no place for us to stay. Luckily, the city opened up its biggest park to campers and we ended up sleeping in Fairmount Park, the wilderness inside Philly.

The next morning, we finally woke up to the big day—July 4th, 1976! When we emerged from our tent, we could already hear the commotion coming from the big parade.

But as we left the park, we wound up in unfamiliar neighborhoods that felt run-down and a bit scary. People sat on their stoops and watched us pass. We kept following the sounds, figuring once we got to the parade, it'd be fine. But this parade wasn't like the one we saw in DC.

Hundreds of people were marching in street clothes and work clothes, holding protest signs and raising their fists. The signs said things like JOBS NOT WAR, POVERTY ISN'T WORTH CELEBRATING, and FREEDOM FOR ALL THE OPPRESSED. I noticed that most of the marchers were Black or brown, Asian or Native American. There were lots of women and kids, too. And none of them were waving the red, white, and blue.

WE'VE CARRIED THE RICH FOR 200 YEARS-
LET'S GET THEM OFF OUR BACKS!

Jobs or Income!
We Won't Fight Another Rich Man's War!
Demonstrate July 4th!

It turns out these people had been having a lot of the same feelings I had about the differences between the words in the Declaration of Independence and the real world we lived in. But they were using their voices to stand up for what they believed in, demanding a better future for themselves and their families. Kind of like the colonists did way back when.

Isn't that the American way?

It turned out this wasn't the big parade we were looking for but was part of a series of protests called the People's Bicentennial. The real parade was in another part of town . . . but by then, I think we'd had enough of parades.

We decided to check out Independence Hall and the Liberty Bell, but the crowds were a little overwhelming, so we just took a quick picture. We were about to leave when we started hearing church bells ringing. They rang for a long time and seemed to be coming from miles all around the city.

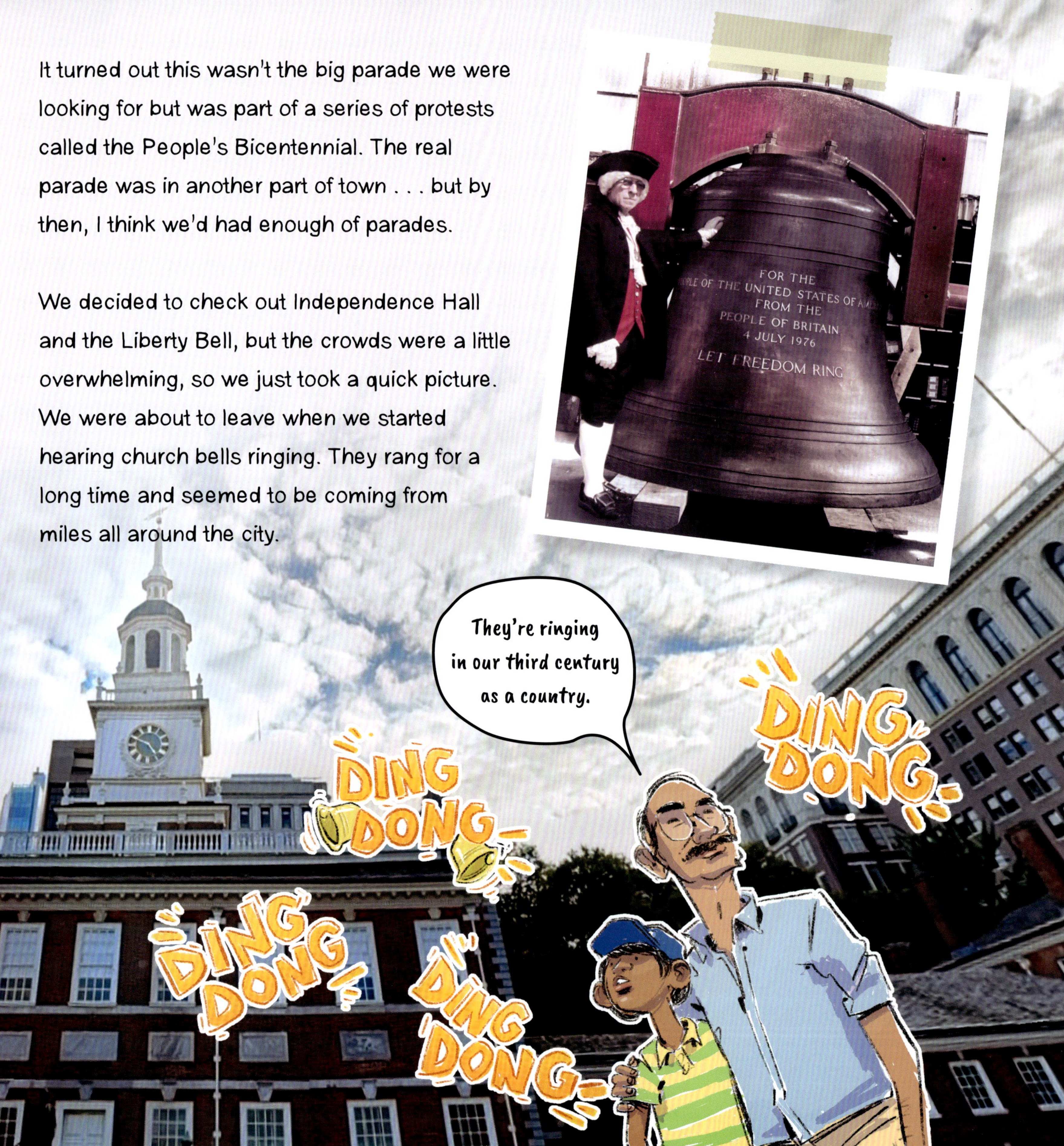

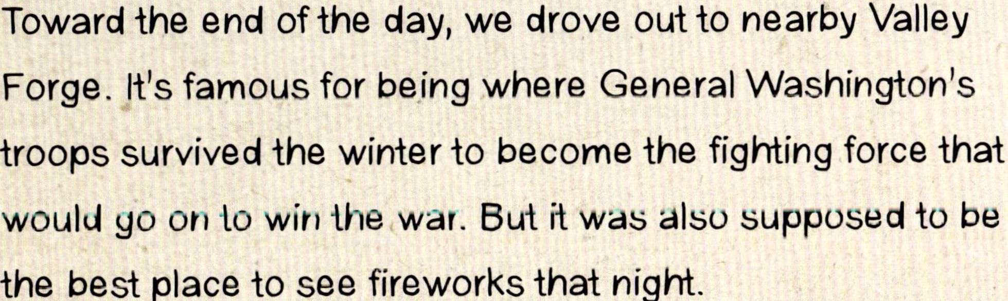

Toward the end of the day, we drove out to nearby Valley Forge. It's famous for being where General Washington's troops survived the winter to become the fighting force that would go on to win the war. But it was also supposed to be the best place to see fireworks that night.

When we came over the hill, we saw the strangest thing: not only a grassy pasture full of people but also a huge caravan of covered wagons! There must have been two hundred of them. It turned out that folks had crossed the country from west to east in these covered horse-drawn wagons, as a tribute to American pioneers. Some took a whole year to get there. And I thought our trip was long!

That night, we found a spot on the grassy hill, and as night fell, the music started and there was a series of thundering BOOMs! Fireworks filled the skies.

We had made it across the whole country for the July 4th Bicentennial! I sat with my mom and dad and my brothers, and we let the whole trip wash over us . . .

The next morning, we left the city in a daze and began our drive home.

The long journey back was like a dream filled with fleeting snapshots. In New York Harbor, we looked out from the crown of the Statue of Liberty at the dozens of special tall ships that filled the harbor.

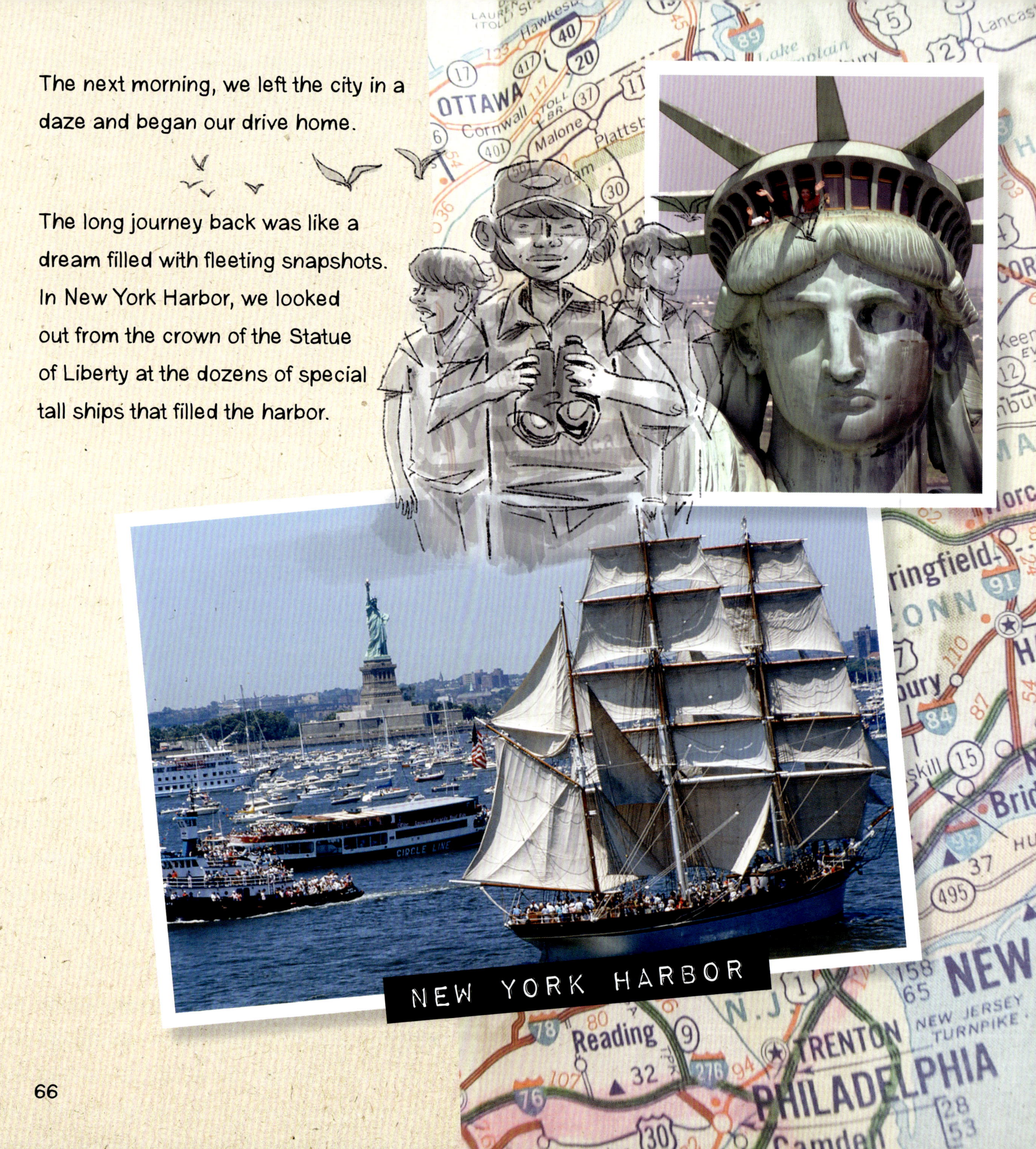

NEW YORK HARBOR

It was all a blur, like a slide show of future memories. Boston. Niagara Falls. The windy city of Chicago. The Gateway Arch in St. Louis. The flatness of Kansas.

Somewhere around the Rocky Mountains, I started thinking back over the last month and a half, about all the monuments and natural wonders we'd seen and the strange encounters, conquests, and scary moments that we'd experienced . . .

Like that time my dad had to chase off a couple of bears that wandered into our camp in the middle of the night!

Or when we were crossing Tornado Alley and alerts started blaring over the radio. We suddenly found ourselves surrounded by tornadoes to the north, east, and south! We kept changing direction to find an escape route, and after several hours, we somehow made it out alive. Whew!

Or that time a pickup truck got struck by lightning right in front of us and drove off the highway!

Or when our car broke down in the middle of nowhere in the South and we flagged down a mean-looking guy in a pickup with a shotgun behind him. But instead of being who I thought he was, he took a look at our engine and said he knew someone who could fix it. It took two days to get fixed and we stayed in our tent behind the mechanic's garage.

Or when we tried to get into New York City through the Holland Tunnel during rush hour in a summer heatwave (later my mom fainted!). We were forced by authorities to turn around—in traffic—because we had a propane tank on our camper. After hearing New Yorkers hate on us for the twenty minutes we blocked the tunnel, my dad started thinking we should just skip New York right there . . .

The last stop on our trip might have been both the least and most American city ever: Las Vegas. The hotel seemed so glamorous after weeks of sleeping in campgrounds. Since it was the last stop before home, we were going to go out in style (giant buffets! pools! Circus Circus!). We even won on a slot machine!

The trip had been a whirlwind, but I was ready for home. Traveling with your family in a small car for seven weeks can be tough at times. Arguments break out over all kinds of silly stuff, and you get sick of sitting next to someone because they farted or ate your last space food stick. Sometimes you just get tired of looking at their face and want to have some alone time.

Along the way, we got flat tires (twice), had a blown head gasket, and got lost more than once. We even got a speeding ticket when Dad was barely doing 58 miles per hour. And setting up that tent and moving luggage around for the millionth time got old real fast.

I think everyone was exhausted (especially my dad, who drove almost the whole way), and I really missed my cat and the beach where we lived.

When we pulled up to our house, we found Scratchy still alive and well, if a little worse for wear. I couldn't wait to race down to the Pacific and dive in. Home, sweet home!

In the following days, as we were recovering from our epic journey, I found myself starting to make new lists for my next American adventures.

As an adult, I've done a few of these things and many others I hadn't thought of then . . .

When I returned to school in September, I had to give a report about what we did over the summer. This is some of what I read out loud to my class:

We sat around campfires, swam in lakes that looked like the ocean, got soaked under Niagara Falls. I touched the Atlantic with my toe. I met a Navajo kid who liked peanut butter and a Mexican boy who rode junior broncos in the rodeo! I ate something called a goober burger—peanut butter on a hamburger! Mmm. We saw America, celebrated its big birthday in Washington, DC, and Philadelphia, and saw all kinds of people from all over the country! I think America is super big. And the people sometimes talk or dress funny but that's okay. We are all trying to get along, even if we are all different.

Today, when I see kids do the Pledge of Allegiance in school, I think about how different things are from when I was a kid in 1976. Things feel much more complicated these days, but the ideas I saw on that trip still mean something—we are all part of this country, and I think we all believe in the ideas on which it was built, even if we disagree about what they mean.

So, in that Spirit of '76, I thought I'd write a new Pledge of Allegiance for our upcoming 250th birthday (the Semiquincentennial!):

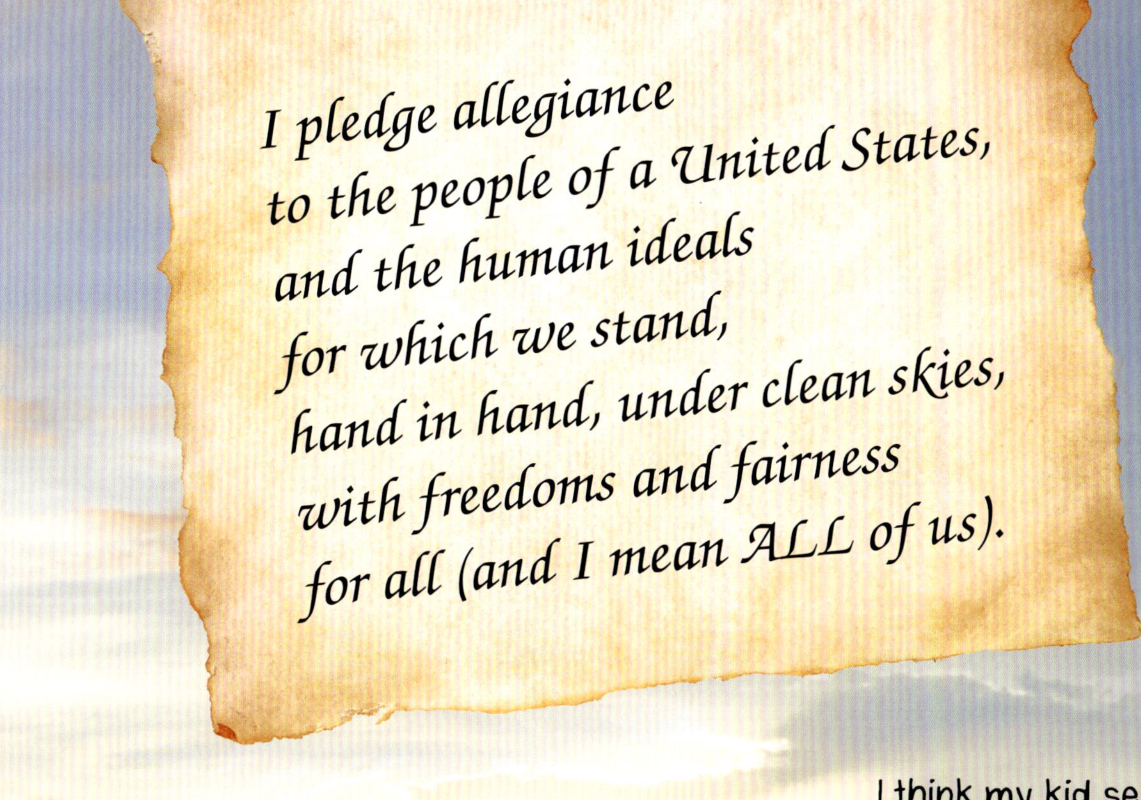

I pledge allegiance
to the people of a United States,
and the human ideals
for which we stand,
hand in hand, under clean skies,
with freedoms and fairness
for all (and I mean ALL of us).

I think my kid self would have liked that.

A NOTE FROM THE AUTHOR

As a children's author, I'm lucky that my job takes me to all kinds of places I never would have visited otherwise, where I get to meet all kinds of people I never would have met. Through research and school visits (and a few vacations), I've now been to forty-eight of the fifty states (excluding Alaska and North Dakota) and all seven continents, including Antarctica. I've lived in Berlin, Vienna, Montreal, Vancouver, Santa Cruz, and Tampa and spent time in Siberia, South Africa, Australia, New Zealand, Mexico, and many parts of eastern and western Europe. But I think it all started for me on that grand expedition in the summer of 1976!

My trip to Antarctica in 2017 opened my eyes to new ways of looking at my travels. Part of my job, I think, is to have these experiences and then write about them to share with you. I am curious about every place I visit, and there's so much to learn, even here in America. Students rarely see their hometown as a place worth visiting or writing about, but to me, every place can be as exotic as Antarctica if you look closely enough. I think that's one of the big takeaways from my Bicentennial trip: It opened my eyes to what's special about where we all live. One of my favorite things is to ask students about their hometown: What is the one food they have there that nobody else eats? What special words do they use? What should I see that's unique to this place? What is the strangest thing they ever saw there?

In 1976, America was in a rut. Maybe all the Bicentennial hype was a way for us to remember our past, even if that past isn't as ideal as we'd like it to be. As President Ford later remarked, "Rarely in the history of the world had so many people turned out so spontaneously to express the love they felt for their country. . . . We had regained our pride . . . and, in doing so, we had laid the foundation for a future that had to be filled with hope."

It was a reminder that as flawed as our nation's founders were, they were reaching for a higher ideal called democracy. And though it will never be even close to perfect, true democracy will always be worth fighting for.

IN MEMORY OF MY DAD
1930–2021

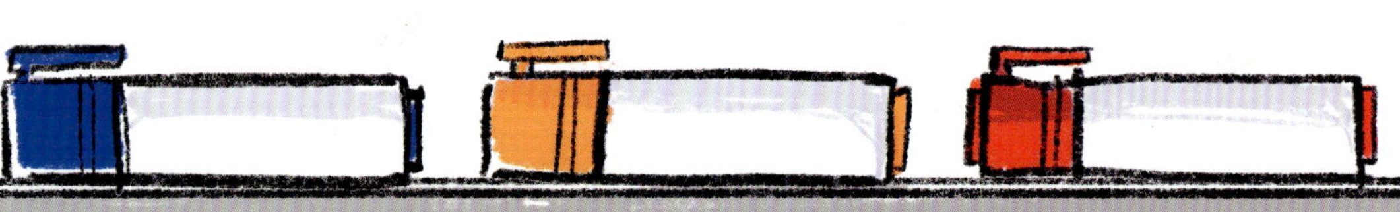

FACTS ABOUT THE UNITED STATES

The United States of America is big. In 1776, there were only 2.5 million British subjects in thirteen colonies. Two hundred years later, there were fifty states and over 200 million people. Today, we have almost 340 million people from places all over the world.

Life expectancy has gone from under forty years old in 1776 to seventy-three in 1976 and over seventy-seven today. In 1776, it took ten days to travel from Philadelphia to Boston by horse. Today, you can fly across the country in five to six hours. The number of vehicles on our roads more than doubled from 1976 to today, and V-8 gas guzzlers are slowly being replaced by long-range electric vehicles.

In 1776, the average yearly salary was about $3,900 in today's dollars. In 1976, it was about $39,000. Today's average is almost $60,000. Fast food in 1776 included pickles and syllabub (cider with curdled whipped cream). A marbles game called ringtaw and ninepin bowling were all the rage, along with drinking and singing. In the 1970s, VCRs, frozen dinners, and video-game arcades were the next big thing. Today, it's TikTok, Grubhub, and Xbox. In 1976, I could see the original *Rocky* in a movie theater for $1.50. Today you can stream *Creed III* on your phone.

Some things haven't grown—families are half the size today than at the time of the Revolutionary War. There are many reasons for this, but the costs of raising a family and the fact that we don't need so many people to work on the family farm anymore are two big ones. Kids go to school instead. Women and members of underrepresented groups can now vote and hold every position of power in the country.

But there is still way too much injustice and inequality. Issues we thought we solved decades ago are being challenged and overturned. Democracy and its freedoms are constantly evolving, and sometimes it's not for the better. Getting involved by voting and raising awareness are vital to protecting our rights as Americans.

Being in a democracy means you can't just complain from the sidelines whenever you don't like something. To be an American means you have to be part of the American Dream, good and bad. So speak up and make sure your voice gets heard!

BIG QUESTIONS
ABOUT AMERICAN HISTORY

What were some of the big conflicts that triggered the Revolutionary War?

The Boston Massacre took place in 1770, when British redcoats opened fire on unarmed civilians who were verbally taunting them.

In 1773, colonists protesting against taxes on British imports dumped imported tea into the harbor, an event that became known as the Boston Tea Party.

Two years later, the "shot heard round the world" marked the beginning of the war as British troops tried to seize the colonial militia's weapons in Concord.

What is the Declaration of Independence?

More than a year into the war, Thomas Jefferson (with the help of some others) wrote the Declaration of Independence to show the king we meant business. It was adopted on July 4, 1776, by fifty-six men who came to be known as the Founding Fathers. That's why July 4th is a big deal!

Who were some of the most famous people from the war?

General George Washington is often credited as the stalwart military leader who won the war. His iconic moments include surviving the winter at Valley Forge, where he retrained his ill-equipped troops to become real fighters, and developing a daring plan to cross the Delaware River on Christmas 1776, in a surprise attack that revitalized the Revolution after many defeats.

Paul Revere was a silversmith turned folk hero because of his midnight ride to alert the colonial militia about approaching British troops before the battles of Lexington and Concord. Patrick Henry was a politician whose call to arms became famous: "I know not what course others may take; but as for me, give me liberty, or give me death!" Nathan Hale was a soldier and spy for the Continental army who was captured and executed by the British.

John Hancock was one of the Founders whose large and stylish signature is the most famous on the Declaration of Independence. Benjamin Franklin was a Founder, printer, scientist, inventor, and our first postmaster general. He was largely responsible for securing France's help in finally winning the war against the British. Betsy Ross was credited with making the first American flag, but this is more folklore than fact. She was an early flag maker at any rate.

Did the Founders enslave people?

Most of the signers of the Declaration owned enslaved people. It was a moral quandary that was argued about, but even many of those who were against enslavement in theory didn't practice what they preached. It would take almost a hundred years, until after the Civil War, for slavery

BENJAMIN FRANKLIN, FOUNDER

to be abolished nationally. However, harsh segregation laws, followed by ongoing problems of inequality and prejudice, have continued to be a stain on our nation's history.

How did the Founders treat Native Americans?

While colonialists were searching for land and freedom, they did so at the expense of those who were already here. The Declaration refers to Native Americans as "merciless Indian savages," and the history of the United States includes many broken promises and grievous injustices against Indigenous peoples and nations.

DEB HAALAND,
US SECRETARY OF THE INTERIOR

When did Black people gain the right to vote?

African American men gained the right to vote in 1870. However, due to intimidation tactics like poll taxes and literacy tests created solely for Black voters, most did not vote until the civil rights movement led to the passage of the Voting Rights Act of 1965, which prohibited racial discrimination in voting.

When did women gain the right to vote?

Women's rights were not part of the Founders' discussion, though John Adams's wife, Abigail, advised him to "remember the ladies." The women's movement for equality began with a convention in 1848, but it wasn't until 1920 that women gained the right to vote nationally.

Why do we say the Pledge of Allegiance in school?

The pledge began as a magazine ad campaign to sell flags in 1892, aimed at the Chicago World's Fair and the 400th anniversary of Columbus reaching America. It was revised and featured in schools, first as a once-a-year event, then daily, in the hope that it would encourage patriotism among immigrants and reinforce our nationhood in the wake of the Civil War. The phrase "under God" wasn't added to the pledge until 1954. Today, forty-seven states require schools to say it every morning, but the Supreme Court ruled in 1943 that students can't be forced to say it.

Who were some of the most famous early American pioneers?

Daniel Boone was an officer in the Revolutionary War who became famous for exploring Kentucky. Tall tales about his life portrayed him as an adventurous explorer who loved to fight and rejected "civilization," though the truth was more complicated than that.

Lewis and Clark led an expedition in the early 1800s from St. Louis to the Pacific Ocean. Their journey wouldn't have been possible without the help of Native American people that they met along the way. Lewis and Clark returned from their trip with information about the geography of the West, as well as its plants and animals, some of which they had never encountered before.

The Donner Party was a group of American pioneers who headed west in a wagon train, ending in a tragic crossing of the Sierra Nevada mountain range in the winter of 1846-1847. Many perished in a ghastly manner.

To Native Americans, these expeditions were devastating, as white American expansion continued to encroach on their lands with catastrophic consequences.

In the early twentieth century, mass migrations grew as people fled severe drought, racism, or economic downturn to seek out new opportunities in the western and northern parts of the country. They were pioneers of a different kind, in search of the American Dream.

What are some famous protests in US history?

Acts of protest such as marches, boycotts, or sit-ins are built into the very fabric of our country. Beginning with the Boston Tea Party in 1773, protests have become as American as apple pie and baseball (though probably more heated). While most people know about the protests to support women's rights and civil rights and to oppose the Vietnam War, those are just the tip of the iceberg.

COXEY'S ARMY, 1894: In 1894, Jacob Coxey led a delegation of ten thousand unemployed Americans to Washington, DC, to pressure Congress to pass a national jobs bill. Although Coxey was arrested before he could deliver his planned speech in front of the Capitol and his gathered "army" dispersed, the press took their side, and the event, considered the first US protest aimed at changing the government's mind, would inspire many in the future to stand up.

UNION STRIKES, 1886–TODAY: Starting with the Great Southwest railroad strike of 1886, trade unions have organized walkouts to demand better wages, hours, and conditions for workers. Labor groups representing railroad workers, steelworkers, coal miners, textile workers, postal workers, and other trades have banded together to force companies to improve their lot. While some strikes resulted in violence and mass firings, many were successful, like the steel strike of 1959, when over half a million workers refused to work in order to fight for higher wages and better benefits. The American labor movement has improved conditions for workers and helped to create a functional middle class.

CHILDREN'S CRUSADE, 1963: In 1963, one thousand students in Birmingham, Alabama, set off to talk to the mayor about issues of segregation in their communities. Many were arrested or had firehoses and dogs turned on them by the police. The events shocked the public and led President Kennedy to officially support a national civil rights bill.

STONEWALL UPRISING, 1969: A police raid on the Stonewall Inn, a popular gay spot in New York City, led to an uprising that lasted six days and helped spark the gay rights movement in the United States. Within a year, three new publications had been launched in the city to report on the struggle for gay rights. Gatherings to commemorate the uprising evolved into LGBTQIA+ pride parades around the country, which have helped to spur great strides, both socially and legally.

WHITE HOUSE PEACE VIGIL/NO NUKES, 1980S: In 1981, activist William Thomas began a peaceful vigil in front of the White House to protest America's nuclear arms race with the Soviet Union. The No Nukes campaign grew national, with protests all over the country, including a 1982 No Nukes

PRESIDENT JOHN F. KENNEDY

gathering in Central Park that drew one million protesters. These protests pushed the two superpowers to negotiate disarmament agreements.

BLACK LIVES MATTER, 2013–TODAY: The deaths of Trayvon Martin and many other African Americans, often at the hands of police, spurred national outrage. Black Lives Matter hit its peak during the COVID pandemic, with 15–25 million people protesting the death of George Floyd. These actions led many cities to reconsider how their police forces are trained and deployed.

STANDING ROCK PROTESTS, 2016: In 2016, young people from the Standing Rock Indian Reservation and other nearby communities joined forces to protest the building of an oil pipeline near their land that threatened their water supply as well as burial sites. Connected by social media, crowds grew to thousands of people from around the country. While the protest did not ultimately stop the pipeline, it helped galvanize a national movement for Native American rights and was the largest gathering of Indigenous people in the United States in over a century.

MARCH FOR OUR LIVES, 2018: Led by a student organization formed after the Parkland high school shooting in 2018, up to two million people hit the streets in support of gun control legislation, making it one of the largest protests in US history.

A. PHILIP RANDOLPH, ACTIVIST

ABOUT TRAVELING THE UNITED STATES

What were the first cross-country trips like?

In 1903, on a $50 bet, Dr. Horatio Jackson, together with his driving partner, Sewall K. Crocker, and a bulldog named Bud, drove from San Francisco to New York in sixty-three days, just to prove he could drive a "horseless carriage" across America! There were no highways—mostly just dirt roads with little signage, and sometimes not even that. A few years later, the Great Auto Race of 1908 (the inspiration for my favorite movie as a kid, *The Great Race*) began in Times Square. Six cars from around the world raced to cross the country in forty-one days—then continued by ship on to Asia and Europe! (The US team won the race.)

How was the National Park System created?

Artist George Catlin suggested in 1832 that the incredible landscapes of the American West could be saved from developers "by some great protecting policy of government . . . A nation's Park, containing man and beast, in all the wild and freshness of their nature's beauty!" Naturalist John Muir is considered the Father of the National Parks, for his writing and activism that showed why such beauty needed to be preserved. In 1872, Yellowstone became the first national park. In 1916, the National Park Service was created to run and maintain the nation's natural treasures.

Who built the US highway system?

In 1956, President Dwight D. Eisenhower began the creation of the US Interstate Highway System, which had been dreamed about since the invention of the automobile. The system cost over $618 billion in today's dollars to build (roughly $15 million a mile) and now covers 48,482 miles of highway, including ten transcontinental highways. By the early 1970s, even with a 400 percent rise in first-time flyers, more than half of all Americans had still never flown in a plane, but most families had a car, and throughout the '70s, Americans drove over 14.4 trillion highway miles, enough to drive around the world more than 578 million times.

Who invented rest stops?

Before long distance road trips became common, people had to pack all their food and eat in or next to their cars on the side of the road. But with better roads being built and scenic interests along the way, engineer Allan Williams decided travelers should have nicer places to rest and eat. In 1929, he had his crews build green lunch tables and benches, creating the first rest stop in Michigan. The idea of serving motorists' needs and interests by the side of the

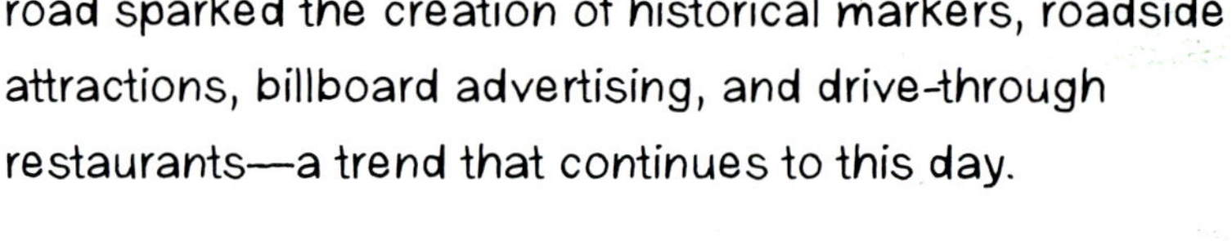

road sparked the creation of historical markers, roadside attractions, billboard advertising, and drive-through restaurants—a trend that continues to this day.

I love America more than any other country in this world, and, exactly for this reason, I insist on the right to criticize her perpetually.

JAMES BALDWIN, AUTHOR

How did Black drivers stay safe on the road?

For African Americans, traveling, especially through the South, was a risky proposition. Sometimes a driver might wear a chauffeur's hat so they wouldn't be pulled over by racist police. For long trips, even stopping for gas could be dangerous. Seeing that something needed to be done to address this problem, New York letter carrier Victor Hugo Green started a guidebook in 1936, called the Green Book, which became "the bible of Black travel" during the years of Jim Crow segregation laws. The guide listed mostly Black-owned motels, restaurants, and stores that would be safe to stop at.

When did the US implement speed limits?

With more and more road travelers driving at high speeds to reach their destinations in good time, accidents and fatalities began to rise. In the 1970s, a 55-mile-per-hour speed limit was set nationwide, lowering highway deaths by 16 percent in the first year. Counties soon benefited from the use of radar guns to clock speeds, as the resulting speeding tickets raised millions of dollars for their budgets. Consumer items like the Fuzzbuster, which detected upcoming speed traps, and CB radios, which allowed truck drivers to alert others about cops hiding behind billboards and trees, became hot-selling items.

Are we there yet?

Cars had fairly poor gas mileage in the '70s, and on lonely stretches of highway, gas stations could be few and far between. Since my dad was an accountant, his job was to calculate the exact mileage of our car, so we could stretch every gallon of gas to the max and not run out in the middle of nowhere. This included driving at slower speeds with no AC for better gas mileage when necessary.

SEAT BELTS: While seat belts were introduced to cars in the mid-1950s, most Americans in the 1970s did not wear them. Kids in station wagons particularly were free to roam between the wayback and the middle seats. Some station wagons had front seats that swiveled around or L-shaped couch seats in the back. It's a miracle we all survived. The first state to make it mandatory to wear a seat belt didn't do so until 1984.

ELEANOR ROOSEVELT, FIRST LADY

What were some of the more unusual sites we visited along the way?

LONDON BRIDGE: This bridge spans Lake Havasu in Arizona. It was constructed from the actual exterior stones of the famous London Bridge, built over the River Thames in the 1830s, then bought by American entrepreneur Robert P. McCulloch in 1968 to create a tourist destination in the desert.

OK CORRAL: The corral became known as the site of a famous gunfight, with lawman Wyatt Earp, Doc Holliday, and others on one side and a cattle-rustling gang called the Cowboys on the other. The battle lasted only a minute but has lived on as legend in movies and books.

METEOR CRATER: At about 4,000 feet in diameter and over 500 feet deep, this is the best-preserved meteorite impact site on earth, found in Winslow, Arizona.

FOUR CORNERS: This is the only place in America where four states meet: Arizona, Utah, Colorado, and New Mexico. A flat monument lies in the middle of nowhere where the states meet; one can stand in the middle and be in four states at once!

PETRIFIED FOREST: Petrified remnants of trees, over 200 million years old, lie across the surreal landscape of the Painted Desert in eastern Arizona.

DEALEY PLAZA: The site of the assassination of President John F. Kennedy in Dallas, Texas, on November 22, 1963.

ROADSIDE ATTRACTIONS: Fiberglass giants called Muffler Men, concrete dinosaurs, and various "world's biggest" items (peanut, ketchup bottle, rocking chair, buffalo, thermometer, and more) pop up in the middle of nowhere to draw tourists to places they'd never stop at along the endless highways of America.

What were some of the biggest and most unusual events of the Bicentennial?

There were several months-long campaigns leading up to July 4, 1976. On TV, there were nightly Bicentennial Minutes, which highlighted moments from the Revolutionary War with an "on this day in history" approach. The American Freedom Train and the Bicentennial Wagon Train Pilgrimage toured the United States and hosted the president to celebrate the nation's independence. New York City hosted an epic parade of tall ships called OpSail, while Philadelphia and Washington held the biggest parades their cities had ever seen. On the afternoon of July 4th, cities around the country rang in the third century of our nation with church bells ringing for three minutes. Almost every city in America hosted parades and fireworks the likes of which this country had never seen.

RECOMMENDED READING

If you want to learn more about the US of A, consider checking out these books:

Eggers, Dave. *What Can a Citizen Do?* Illustrated by Shawn Harris. Chronicle Books, 2018.

Hale, Nathan. Hazardous Tales series. Abrams, 2012–2023.

Long, Michael G. *Kids on the March: 15 Stories of Speaking Out, Protesting, and Fighting for Justice*. Algonquin, 2021.

Messner, Kate. History Smashers series. Random House, 2021–2024.

Ray, Richard. *Don't Make Me Pull Over! An Informal History of the Family Road Trip*. Scribner, 2018.

Reynolds, Jason, and Ibram X. Kendi. *Stamped (for Kids): Racism, Antiracism, and You*. Adapted by Sonja Cherry-Paul. Little, Brown, 2021.

Sorell, Traci. *We Are Still Here! Native American Truths Everyone Should Know*. Illustrated by Frané Lessac. Charlesbridge, 2021.

Tarshis, Lauren. *I Survived the American Revolution, 1776*. Scholastic, 2017.

SOURCE NOTES

epigraph: "It is probably a pity . . . of America": Dwight D. Eisenhower, "Remarks at the Vermont State Dairy Festival, Rutland, Vermont, June 22, 1955, https://www.presidency.ucsb.edu/documents/remarks-the-vermont-state-dairy-festival-rutland-vermont.

p. 78: "Rarely in the history . . . hope": Gerald R. Ford, *A Time to Heal* (Harper and Row, 1979), 393.

p. 80: "shot heard round the world": Ralph Waldo Emerson, "Concord Hymn," in *Selected Writings (*Simon and Schuster, 2010), 335–336.

p. 80: "I know not what course . . . death!": Patrick Henry, "Give Me Liberty or Give Me Death," March 23, 1775, Yale Law School Avalon Project, https://avalon.law.yale.edu/18th_century/patrick.asp.

p. 80: "Where liberty dwells, there is my country": Although this statement is widely attributed to Benjamin Franklin, a definitive source has not been found. It's an English version of the Latin motto *Ubi libertas, ibi patria.*

p. 81: "remember the ladies": Abigail Adams to John Adams, March 31, 1776, Massachusetts Historical Society, https://www.masshist.org/digitaladams/archive/doc?id=L17760331aa.

p. 81: "Every day we should stop . . . the country": Deb Haaland, "Honoring My Ancestors," Medium, November 21, 2017, https://medium.com/@deb4congressnm/honoring-my-ancestors-710065e7cb5a.

p. 82: "Ask not . . . your country": John F. Kennedy, Inaugural Address (1961), National Archives, https://www.archives.gov/milestone-documents/president-john-f-kennedys-inaugural-address.

p. 83: "Freedom . . . is won": A. Philip Randolph, *For Jobs and Freedom: Selected Speeches and Writings of A. Philip Randolph*, ed. Andrew E. Kersten and David Lucander (University of Massachusetts Press 2014), 100.

p. 83: "by some great . . . nature's beauty!": George Catlin, *Letters and Notes on the Manners, Customs, and Condition of the North American Indians* (n.p., 1841), 261–262.

p. 84: "I love America . . . perpetually": James Baldwin, *Notes of a Native Son* (Beacon Press, 1955), 9.

p. 85: "True patriotism . . . on earth": Eleanor Roosevelt, *Book of Common Sense Etiquette* (Macmillan, 1962), 550.

p. 93: "America is not the project . . . belongs to everyone": Barack Obama, "Remarks at the 50th Anniversary of the Selma to Montogomery Marches," March 7, 2015, https://obamawhitehouse.archives.gov/the-press-office/2015/03/07/remarks-president-50th-anniversary-selma-montgomery-marches.

PHOTO CREDITS

All photos by G. Neri, except historical photos found in public domain or credited below. Many thanks to the Library of Congress, the National Parks Service Photo Gallery, the Ronald Reagan and Gerald Ford Libraries, NARA Public Domain Archives, the National Archives, the New York Public Library, Temple University Library, NASA, Flickr and Wikimedia Commons, and the Environmental Protection Agency's DOCUMERICA project.

Endpapers: July 4th poster: Library of Congress, Prints & Photographs Division, LC-USZC4-8134; pre-title quote on billboard: Kevin Payravi, Wikimedia Commons, CC BY-SA 4.0, https://creativecommons.org/licenses/by-sa/4.0/

pp. 4–5: photo of G. Neri in Antarctica: courtesy Kirsten Carlson; G. Neri with microphone: courtesy Brian Steblen/Nazareth University; amazed reader: courtesy Stephanie Bell

p. 8: Vietnam protest: UW Collections, CC BY 2.0, https://creativecommons.org/licenses/by/2.0

pp. 8–9: Twins copyright © ASSOCIATED PRESS; bicentennial cake copyright © ASSOCIATED PRESS

p. 12: Ronald Reagan leading pledge: courtesy Ronald Reagan Library
p. 24: Crater: Patrick Rohe, CC BY-ND 2.0, https://creativecommons.org/licenses/by-nd/2.0/; London Bridge: Roman Eugeniusz, CC BY-SA, 3.0, https://creativecommons.org/licenses/by-sa/3.0/; OK Corral: P,TO 19104, CC BY-SA 4.0, https://creativecommons.org/licenses/by-sa/4.0/
pp. 32–33: Lincoln Highway ad: Carl Wycoff, CC BY 2.0, https://creativecommons.org/licenses/by/2.0/; license plates: Techa Tungateja/iStock
p. 37: KOA campground: Jasperdo, CC BY-NC-ND 2.0, https://creativecommons.org/licenses/by-nc-nd/2.0/; dust bowl: from the New York Public Library
p. 40: Slave Haven sign: Jimmy Quick, CC BY-NC-SA 2.0, https://creativecommons.org/licenses/by-nc-sa/2.0/
p. 41: Confederate flag: Thomas R. Machnitzki, CC BY 3.0, https://creativecommons.org/licenses/by/3.0/
p. 46: Car stack: Library of Congress, Prints & Photographs Division, photograph by Carol M. Highsmith, LC-DIG-highsm-04367; hat building: Library of Congress, Prints & Photographs Division, photograph by John Margolies, LC-DIG-mrg-00006; Muffler Man: Library of Congress, Prints & Photographs Division, photograph by John Margolies, LC-DIG-mrg-05643
p. 48: Frog legs: Gertjan R., CC BY-SA 3.0, https://creativecommons.org/licenses/by-sa/3.0; pig brain sandwich: Tim Schapker, CC BY 2.0, https://creativecommons.org/licenses/by/2.0/; hot beef sundae: Matt Stoller, CC BY 2.0, https://creativecommons.org/licenses/by/2.0/
p. 49: Eagle: Andy Morffew, CC BY 2.0, https://creativecommons.org/licenses/by/2.0/; Amish buggies: Library of Congress, Prints & Photographs Division, photograph by Carol M. Highsmith, LC-DIG-highsm-14688
p. 50: Yorktown: Steven C. Berger, CC BY-SA 3.0, https://creativecommons.org/licenses/by-sa/3.0/
p. 51: Washington Monument: Sean Pavone/iStock
p. 52: Jefferson Memorial: Joeravi/iStock
p. 53: Poster: Library of Congress, Prints & Photographs Division, LC-DIG-ppmsca-59405
p. 58: Crowd with flag © Darrell C. Crain, Jr., courtesy DC Public Library, The People's Archive, p35 Darrell C. Crain, Jr. Photograph Collection, 1976 Bicentennial Fireworks
p. 59: Fairmount Park: Library of Congress, Prints & Photographs Division, photograph by Carol M. Highsmith, LC-DIG-highsm-15368
p. 60: People's parade courtesy of the Special Collections Research Center. Temple University Libraries. Philadelphia, PA.
p. 61: Poster: Washington Area Spark, CC BY-NC 2.0, https://creativecommons.org/licenses/by-nc/2.0/

PRESIDENT BARACK OBAMA

p. 63: President Ford: courtesy Ford Library Museum; Valley Forge crowd: © ASSOCIATED PRESS
p. 66: Statue of Liberty: courtesy Ronald Reagan Library; New York Harbor: Library of Congress, Prints & Photographs Division, photograph by Bernard Gotfryd, LC-DIG-gtfy-04876
p. 67: Boston: Lee Wright, CC BY-SA 2.0, https://creativecommons.org/licenses/by-sa/2.0/; Chicago: Josh Hallett, CC BY-SA 2.0, https://creativecommons.org/licenses/by-sa/2.0
p. 68: Tornado: Justin1569 at English Wikipedia, CC BY-SA 3.0, https://creativecommons.org/licenses/by-sa/3.0/
p. 70: Sign: Library of Congress, Prints & Photographs Division, photograph by Carol M. Highsmith, LC-DIG-highsm-12610
p. 76: Pledge: U.S. Army Garrison Yongsan, CC BY-NC-S 2.0, https://creativecommons.org/licenses/by-nc-sa/2.0/
Endpapers: button: Washington Area Spark, CC BY-NC 2.0, https://creativecommons.org/licenses/by-nc/2.0/; Betsy Ross: Library of Congress, Music Division; Grand Canyon: Library of Congress, Prints & Photographs Division, WPA Poster Collection, LC-DIG-ppmsca-1339; Drive Carefully: Terry Hassan, CC BY-NC-SA 2.0, https://creativecommons.org/licenses/by-nc-sa/2.0/

The appearance of US Department of Defense (DoD) visual information does not imply or constitute DoD endorsement.

WE'VE CARRIED THE RICH FOR 200 YEARS-
LET'S GET THEM OFF OUR BACKS
Demonstrate in
Philly
July 1-4
DRIVE
CAREFULLY
Come Back
SOON
YESCO
BET
DEAR M
SEE AMERICA
UNITED STATES TRAVEL BUREAU
MADE BY WORKS PROGRESS ADMINISTRATION FEDERAL ART PROJECT NYC